Let's Investigate Slippery, Splendid Sea Creatures

Madelyn Wood Carlisle

Illustrated by Yvette Santiago Banek

BARRON'S

All inquiries should be addressed to:
Barron's Educational Series, Inc.
250 Wireless Boulevard
Hauppauge, NY 11788

International Standard Book No. 0-8120-4974-8

Library of Congress Catalog Card No. 92-45206

Library of Congress Cataloging-in Publication Data

Carlisle, Madelyn Wood.
  Let's investigate slippery, splendid sea creatures / Madelyn Wood Carlisle;
  illustration by Yvette Santiago Banek.
    p.   cm.
  Includes index.
  Summary: Presents the lives and characteristics of such sea creatures as
  whales, sharks, seals, and corals.
  ISBN 0-8120-4974-8
  1. Marine fauna—Juvenile literature.   [1. Marine animals.]   I. Banek, Yvette
  Santiago, ill.   II. Title.
  QL122.2.C37   1993
  591.92—dc20   92-45206
                                                                           CIP
                                                                            AC

PRINTED IN HONG KONG

3456   9927   987654321

Contents

Whales

The biggest creatures that have ever lived on our planet are alive today! They are the mighty blue whales. The largest of the long-extinct dinosaurs were only half the size of these giants of the deep.

How many full-grown elephants do you think it would take to equal the weight of one adult blue whale? The answer is surprising. At least 30! One captured blue whale was found to be over 110 feet (33 meters) long and to weigh more than 400,000 pounds (181,440 kilograms)!

Whales are not fish. They are mammals. They are more closely related to you than they are to their fishy ocean neighbors. They breathe air, have skulls and spinal columns, and even have finger-like bones in their flippers. Mother whales give birth to live babies and nurse them with milk so rich that baby whales gain as much as 7 pounds (3 kilograms) a day.

If you live near a seacoast, or have vacationed along ocean shores, you may have seen a whale's tail or fin breaking the water's surface, or the spout of steam a whale makes when its warm breath comes in contact with cool air. During the proper season, schools of whales can be seen on their migration to either warmer or colder waters.

The largest dinosaur was only half the size of a blue whale.

4

Sound waves travel far in water and whales keep in touch with each other with a variety of sounds. The most amazing whale sounds are those they use in their songs. Unlike birds, which sing the same songs over and over again, whales compose new ones. The songs of humpback whales are sometimes a half hour long. These whales even seem to have hit tunes. One season all of them, in all the world's oceans, will sing the same song. The next year they might have a new favorite.

In the past, hundreds of thousands of whales were killed for their oil and for other substances their bodies contained. Today many countries have passed laws that limit the number of whales that can be taken from the sea. Nobody wants these wonderful creatures to become extinct.

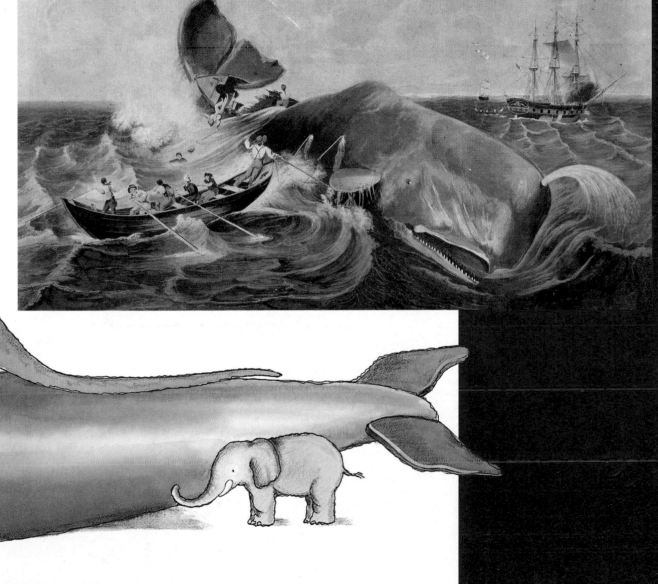

Dolphins

Of all the creatures in the sea, dolphins are the ones most friendly to humans. Dolphins seem to like people and to enjoy their company. Some dolphins will let swimmers come up to them, stroke them, even ride on their backs. Dolphins sometimes come close to beaches and frolic with children.

Many stories are told about dolphins that have helped people in trouble. Swimmers have said they were saved from drowning by dolphins who towed them to shallow water where they could then make it safely ashore. Some marine biologists have said it is almost as if dolphins know that human beings are fellow mammals.

Dolphins live in all the world's oceans. The kind you have probably seen most often, in pictures if not in person, is the bottle-nosed dolphin. This dolphin always looks as if it is smiling. Sometimes it is hard to tell dolphins apart from their very close cousins, the porpoises. And some creatures that we call whales are really dolphins. The big black and white killer whales that perform at marine amusement parks are actually a kind of dolphin.

Dolphins locate food and objects in the water by sending out sounds that bounce back to them. To human ears these sound like clicks and whistles.

The bottle-nosed dolphin always seems to be smiling.

Dolphins enjoy frolicking near ships at sea.

There are many aquariums and marine parks where you can watch trained dolphins perform. They jump through hoops, ring bells, and even throw balls. To learn all these tricks, dolphins taken from the sea are actually sent to school—special places where trainers work with them for many months. Dolphins are very intelligent. They are smarter than dogs, scientists say, and may be as intelligent as chimpanzees. Some dolphins have been taught to make sounds that are a lot like words spoken by their trainers. A dolphin has a brain larger than yours and can learn fast, but no dolphin will ever be able to learn as much as you can.

Dolphins can be trained to perform amazing stunts.

It may be called a "killer whale," but it's really a harmless dolphin.

A friendly dolphin gets a pat on the nose.

Is each animal with a larger brain more intelligent than another kind of animal with a smaller brain? Look at the two columns of drawings below.

The column on the left shows various creatures, sized by the sizes of their brains. Of the animals shown, the sperm whale has the largest brain. Next in brain size is the dolphin, then the human, and, finally, a gorilla and a chimpanzee.

Now study the right-hand column. It shows the same creatures in the order of their intelligence, with the smartest at the top. Even though it has the biggest brain, the sperm whale is the least intelligent. Smarter than the whale is the gorilla, the chimp, and then the dolphin. Of course, the human being is the most intelligent of all.

Sharks

If someone asked you to draw a picture of a shark, you would probably show it looking fierce, ready to attack something or somebody. You might draw its huge jaws wide open, its sharp pointed teeth ready to clamp down on its victim.

It's true that a lot of sharks are dangerous. You wouldn't want to be swimming in water where you knew there were such sharks. What you may not know is that most sharks aren't dangerous at all. There are over 300 different kinds of sharks and most of them have never hurt a human being.

Not all sharks are big either. There's one shark that is only 4 inches (10 centimeters) long! Isn't it odd that this tiny shark has the longest name of any creature of the sea? It is called *Tsuranagahobitozami*. That's a Japanese word that means "dwarf shark with a long face." You can pronounce it by saying *soo-ruh-nah-gah-ho-bee-toe-zah-me*. None of the syllables should be accented more than the others.

The biggest of all sharks is the whale shark. It can weigh as much as 90,000 pounds (40,824 kilograms). The largest whale shark ever measured was caught in the Indian Ocean many years ago. It was almost 61 feet

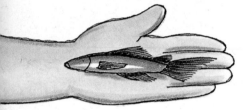

There's a kind of shark that's so small you could easily hold one in the palm of your hand.

The largest sharks are bigger than many whales.

(19 meters) long, which is bigger than most whales. The whale shark is the biggest fish in the world. The second largest fish, the basking shark, can be as much as 40 feet (12 meters) long.

There are many strange sharks. The swell shark, found near New Zealand, barks like a dog. A shark called the spring dogfish glows in the dark with a bright greenish light. The hammerhead shark's head really is shaped like the head of a hammer. The Port Jackson shark lays the most unusual eggs in the world. They are twisted, like corkscrews.

It's easy to see why this is called a "black-tip shark" . . .

. . . and why this spotted one is known as a "leopard shark."

Whether they are big or small, dangerous or harmless, almost all sharks have to keep moving. If they stop, they sink. Other fish have an air bladder, a kind of inner balloon that helps them float. Most sharks don't have this kind of a built-in life preserver. So hour after hour, day after day, year in and year out, they must keep on swimming.

Octopuses and Squids

Most people think that squids and octopuses are even more frightening than sharks. They look fearsome, all right, the octopus with its eight arms, the squid with its ten. And there are reports of divers, even small boats, being attacked by these strange creatures.

Yet the famous ocean explorer, Jacques-Yves Cousteau, says that octopuses are shy, and even playful. It's true that they will try to stay hidden from people. But sometimes, particularly if they are attracted by something bright and shiny, they will wrap one or more of their arms around a diver or swimmer. Those arms are very strong and it's not easy to convince an octopus that it should let go.

Octopuses and squids are more closely related to snails than they are to fish. They inhabit all the world's seas, but are more numerous in places where the water is warm.

Here are some other fascinating facts about octopuses and squids:

- The smallest octopus is only 2 inches (5 centimeters) across. The biggest one ever measured was found

Would you dare grab a squid, as this diver is doing?

washed up on a beach in Florida. The distance from the tip of one arm to the tip of an opposite one was 200 feet (61 meters)!

- The flying squid can leap 20 feet (6 meters) out of the water and glide through the air for 60 yards (55 meters). Some have given sailors the scare of their lives by landing on the decks of ships.

- An octopus can stretch out its arms and its soft, sack-like body until they are as thin as a rubber band. Divers have been astonished to see large octopuses squeeze through tiny cracks between rocks.

- An octopus is a home-loving creature. If it can't find a cozy place to live, such as a hollow under an overhanging rock, it will make one. With its long arms, it gathers stones, shells, pieces of metal and plastic, tin cans, even old tires that have been dumped into the ocean, and actually builds itself an underwater house.

MYTHICAL MONSTERS

For centuries, people have told tales of scary monsters that live in the world's oceans. Could any of these stories be true? Scientists admit that there may be forms of marine life that have not yet been identified, or even seen. However, they also say that most strange sights reported by seamen and others can be explained away. Any of the scary monsters could be:

- A line of dolphins. When they come up to breathe, one after the other, they can look like a sea serpent.
- A pair of sharks, swimming one behind the other, appearing to be one long sea creature.
- Giant squids swimming close to the surface. Particularly frightening is the sight of a squid or octopus with its tentacles wrapped around a whale.
- Marine worms, which can be 45 feet (14 meters) long.
- Eels or sea snakes.
- A group of seabirds, flying in a line just above the water.
- Or even just a mass of seaweed.

With its eight long arms, a large octopus can be pretty scary.

Sea Horses

The little sea horse, which is found in many of the world's warm coastal waters, swims as no other sea creature does, in a vertical position, with its head up and its tail down. It also likes to travel vertically, going smoothly up and down like an elevator. Its eyes are independent of each other so that it can look in two directions at once. And it's the only fish that can hold onto something with its tail. It can twist it around a stalk of seaweed and even swing from weed to weed underwater as a monkey swings from tree to tree in the jungle.

Many sea horses are brightly colored. They can be red, yellow, orange, or green. They can also change their color. If an orange sea horse swims into a bed of green seaweed, it will change its color to green so that hungry bigger fish will have a hard time seeing it.

Most sea horses are tiny. The biggest kind is 1 foot (30 centimeters) long. The smallest is only 1½ inches (4 centimeters) long when it is fully grown. Baby sea horses are born in an unusual way. The mother lays her eggs on the father's abdomen. He forms his pelvic fins into a pouch and carries the eggs for 25 days. When they hatch, hundreds of tiny sea horses, each only a fraction of an inch long, swim out into their watery world.

The sea horse always swims in a vertical position.

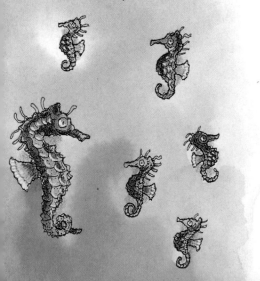

These sea horses have wrapped their tails around a stalk of seaweed.

Sea Cows

On one of his voyages to America, Christopher Columbus saw a creature he didn't recognize swimming in the ocean. What could it be? Some of the men on his ship said it was a mermaid. Of course, mermaids were never real creatures. Thousands of years ago people living around the Mediterranean Sea made up stories about mermaids. They said they were half woman, half fish.

Would *you* ever think these roly-poly creatures were mermaids?

They may look clumsy, but sea cows are graceful swimmers.

When Columbus got a closer look at the strange sea creature, he realized he was seeing something not found in European waters. Later, the newly discovered animal came to be called a sea cow. Sea cows, which live in warm, shallow waters, certainly don't look like mermaids, but they're nothing like cows either. They are called sea cows because they are mammals and mothers nurse their babies. One kind of sea cow, the manatee, lives in the bays and rivers of Florida. It grows to be 13 feet (4 meters) long and can weigh as much as 1,500 pounds (680 kilograms).

A sea cow's snout has two nostrils, which are always closed when the animal is underwater. Every few minutes a sea cow must come up to the surface to breathe.

When a sea cow calf is born, its mother lifts it onto her back with her flippers and takes it up for its first breath.

13

Seals and Sea Lions

Seals are shaped like submarines, only fatter in the middle. They have flippers, two in front, two in back. And they all have long hairs on their faces, sort of like cats' whiskers. There are many different kinds of seals. The largest kind is the elephant seal, and it's easy to see why it got its name. It has a funny-looking trunk.

Have you ever watched an inchworm crawling on a twig, hunching itself up in the middle and then straightening out its front to move forward? That's the way a seal sometimes moves on land. At other times it might pull itself along, using just its front flippers. The rear flippers, which help it to swim in the water, are useless on land. That is why, when seals move around on a beach or a rocky island, places where they like to lie and sun themselves, they look very clumsy. However, if you could dive down into a seal's watery world you would see what a swift and graceful swimmer it is.

You could also tell, by the way it swims, if it is a true seal or a sea lion. A true seal uses its rear flippers, waving them from side to side, to move itself through the water. Its front flippers just help it steer. A sea lion does just the opposite. It uses its rear flippers for steering and its front flippers like paddles.

This young sea lion looks as if he'd like to play.

A mother harbor seal affectionately rubs noses with her pup.

Seals and sea lions can be taught to do many tricks.

14

Many sea lions live close to the shores of Australia, South America, and the western United States. In California, they have become so tame that they often come right up onto docks and piers.

Seals and sea lions are mammals that are closely related

to each other, but you wouldn't have to see them swimming to be able to tell them apart. If the animals you were watching were moving around on shore, you could tell which they were by the way they move. Sea lions do not wriggle forward like inchworms. They bring their rear flippers forward and walk on them. They look like huge feet. And if you saw a male sea lion walking on a beach you could see why it got the lion part of its name. It has a furry mane on its head and neck.

Fur seals look a lot like sea lions, but fur seals have much longer, thicker fur. That is why these beautiful creatures are compared to another one of our familiar land animals. They are often called sea bears.

Sea Otters

Sea otters are playful, web-footed mammals that live close to shore off the western coast of North America, from the Aleutian Islands to California. They spend a lot of their time either grooming their sleek, dark fur or searching for food. If you ate as much, in proportion to your weight, as a sea otter does you might eat 20 pounds (9 kilograms) or more of food a day!

A sea otter often dives deep to find the crabs, sea urchins, small octopuses, and shellfish it likes to eat. Once it has found a meal, it rises to the surface of the water, turns over onto its back, and starts to eat, bringing the food to its mouth with its small, hand-like front paws.

A sea otter has no trouble crushing the soft shells of sea urchins and crabs with its strong teeth, but when the food it wants is encased in a hard, tightly closed shell, the sea otter has a problem. However, it is a problem the clever sea otter has found a way to solve. If you ever have a chance to watch sea otters, either in the ocean or at an aquarium, you might see one of the most amazing and amusing sights of

the animal world. There are very few creatures on our planet that use tools. The sea otter is one of them.

One of the favorite foods of these sleek brown creatures of the sea are the shellfish that grow by the thousands on the sea floor. The hard shells of these creatures must somehow be cracked open before the otter can enjoy its dinner.

So what does the sea otter do? When it picks up a shellfish it also picks up a flat rock. Once the sea otter has come up to the surface and is on its back, it places the rock on its chest and pounds the shellfish against the rock until it cracks open.

Sometimes a sea otter uses rocks in a different way. If it finds a tasty meal fastened to something on the sea floor, it will knock it off by using a stone as a hammer.

Sea otters playing off the California coast.

SEA ZOO

A lot of sea creatures have been named after land animals. In addition to sea horses, sea cows, sea lions, and sea otters, there are:
Butterflyfish
Catfish
Cowfish
Dogfish
Frogfish
Goatfish
Goosefish
Hawkfish
Lionfish
Lizardfish
Parrotfish
Scorpionfish
Squirrelfish
Toadfish
Turkeyfish
Wolffish

Catfish

Goosefish

Lionfish

Wolffish

Sea Turtles

Someday, if you are a passenger on a big ocean liner far out in the middle of the ocean, you might see a large sea turtle swimming along beside the ship. Perhaps you would wonder where it came from and how it got so far from land. The truth is that sea turtles don't care much about dry land. They spend all their time roving Earth's warmer seas. The only time they venture onto a beach is when it's time for the females to lay their eggs. Then they may make very long journeys to return to the same beach where they themselves first crawled out of their eggs and hurried to get into the water.

How do they find their way back to just the right beach? Scientists believe that they navigate over great distances just the way humans have always done, by using the sun and stars to help them find their way from place to place.

Some turtles don't seem to have much choice about where they go. Or maybe they just like traveling the easy way. They can get into an ocean current like the Gulf Stream and be swept along for thousands of miles. Biologists studied some turtles that were found on beaches in England and decided that they had come all the way from the waters of Mexico or the southern United States. How could the scientists be so sure? Because on the turtles' shells was a kind of algae that grows only in the Gulf of Mexico.

Sea turtles swim long distances underwater.

As soon as young sea turtles hatch, they scurry toward the water.

All turtles are good swimmers. You may have seen freshwater turtles in a river or lake. They move through the water by using their flippers as paddles. Sea turtles swim in a different way, holding their flippers still and just moving their feet. They glide through the water in much the same way that an airborne glider floats in the sky, traveling at speeds up to 20 miles (32 kilometers) an hour.

It doesn't take much energy to travel this way. Even a giant leatherback turtle, which can weigh almost 2,000 pounds (907 kilograms), can keep swimming day after day, week after week, for its entire life. And its life is a long one. Sea turtles live longer than any other creatures on Earth. Some have been known to swim the world's oceans for 200 years!

Scientists believe that sea turtles find their way by observing the sun and stars.

Crabs

If you have ever watched a crab running along a beach, you probably laughed at the way it moved, running sideways. Of the world's 4,500 kinds of crabs, there is one that moves in an even stranger fashion. It is the sandbug, the smallest of all crabs, only $\frac{1}{10}$ inch (3 millimeters) long. It does not travel sideways. It doesn't move forward either. Whether it is walking, digging, or swimming, it moves only backwards!

Crabs have five pairs of legs. They walk and run on the four back pairs. The front pair ends in claw-like nippers. These front claws have different shapes in different kinds of crabs.

Have you ever been on a beach or a muddy salt marsh and wondered about the many small holes you see in the sand? They may have been the burrows of fiddler crabs. If you look carefully you might see one, sitting at the entrance to its home for the day. If it is waving its fiddle-shaped claw, you will know it is a male and that he is hoping a female fiddler will come along and like his looks enough to become his mate.

Some small crabs live inside the shells of other sea creatures.

If you caught a crab, would you throw it back or take it home for dinner?

Whereas the little fiddler comes ashore and burrows into the sand, many crabs spend all their time in the water. There they have some odd ways of finding safe places to live. The mussel crab dwells inside the shells of mussels, the oyster crab in the shells of living oysters. Because the

hind part of a hermit crab is soft and not protected by a shell, this crab looks for the empty shell of some other sea creature and backs into it. It staggers along the sea floor, carrying its new home as best it can. When it grows too big for one shell, it searches for a larger one.

One of the most comical things about crabs is the way some disguise themselves to escape their enemies. On their backs they put seaweed, bits of algae, pieces of sponge, small shells, and pebbles.

There's nothing funny about the giant Japanese spider crab, which, as you may have guessed, lives in the waters off Japan. Even though it isn't dangerous unless molested, you wouldn't want to meet up with one of these frightening monsters. Their bodies are as big as a man's and their long legs stretch out over 12 feet (4 meters)!

Jellyfish

When sunlight shines on and through the bodies and tentacles of jellyfish, they glow with such rainbow-like colors that many people think they are the most beautiful of all sea creatures. There are thousands of different kinds of jellyfish. One kind is smaller than a pea. Another measures 8 feet (2 meters) across its body.

All jellyfish have tentacles, long transparent ribbons that dangle below their bodies. One kind has tentacles 400 feet (122 meters) long trailing out behind it as it moves through the water. Plankton, a favorite food, catches on the tentacles of jellyfish and is then carried up to the mouth on the underside of its body.

If you are ever swimming in the ocean and see a jellyfish, you should swim in the opposite direction. Its tentacles could give you a very itchy rash. Some kinds of jellyfish can do a lot more harm than that. The sea wasp jellyfish, found near Australia, gives off a poison stronger than that of any snake. If its tentacles even touch another living creature, the victim will die in a few hours.

Isn't it strange that such a beautiful creature is the most poisonous animal to be found either on land or in the sea?

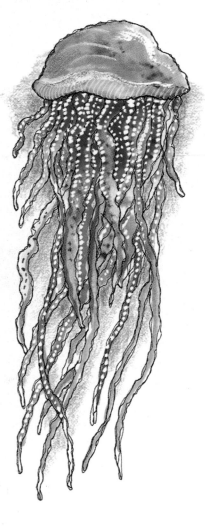

All jellyfish have long, ribbon-like tentacles.

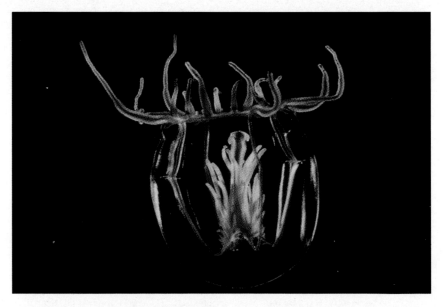

A Medusa jellyfish, one of the sea's most beautiful creatures.

Starfish

There are over 3,000 kinds of starfish and most of them are beautiful to look at. But that's about the only good thing most people have to say about them. We do not eat starfish and so we object to their gobbling up creatures that we do like to eat, such as oysters and clams. Of course, starfish have just as much right to eat an oyster as we do, but there's something about the way they go about it that we humans find disturbing.

A starfish wanders slowly along the sea floor until it comes across something edible. If that something is an oyster or a clam, the starfish places some of its rays, or legs, on one side of the shell and the rest on the other side. Little suction cups on the bottoms of the rays hold tight to the shell. Then the starfish starts to pull, trying to get the shell open.

The creature inside holds out as long as it can, but eventually the shell opens. Just a tiny crack, but it is all the starfish needs. It eats like no other creature in nature. It sticks its whole stomach out through a tiny opening on its underside. The inside-out stomach squeezes into the shell, surrounds the meaty shellfish, digests it, and then pulls back into the body of the starfish.

Starfish live in all the world's seas. This one likes the colder waters of the Pacific Ocean.

Glowing Fish

If you could go down in a special kind of craft called a submersible, into the deepest depths of the sea, you would find yourself in a place never reached by the light of the sun. Yet you would see light, for in that inky blackness, far below the surface of the water, many sea creatures make their own bright light.

Biologists say that 90 percent of the animals at depths lower than 2,500 feet (762 meters) create light. Nine hundred feet (274 meters) down, scientists used a light meter to measure the sunlight that penetrated to that depth during the daytime. Then at night they measured the light made there by the glowing sea creatures. The light from the sea creatures was greater.

The fishy lights are made by special body organs called photophores. Some creatures are lighted all the time. Others can turn their lights on and off. Most of the fish, squid, and other sea animals that glow give off a yellow light, but some shine in brilliant colors. On the sides of the lantern fish there are upper rows of lights that are red, blue, and violet, and lower rows that are red and orange. It even has red tail lights!

Some fish use their lights to blind their enemies. Some use them as a means of identification, so that they can quickly recognize others of their own kind. Others use their lights to attract mates. For some fish their lights act as lures that help them catch other fish. The dragon fish, for instance, dangles lighted globes beneath its body. The kinds of smaller fish it likes to eat are attracted by the globes. And, of course, some fish use their lights the same way you use a flashlight, just to find their way around in the dark.

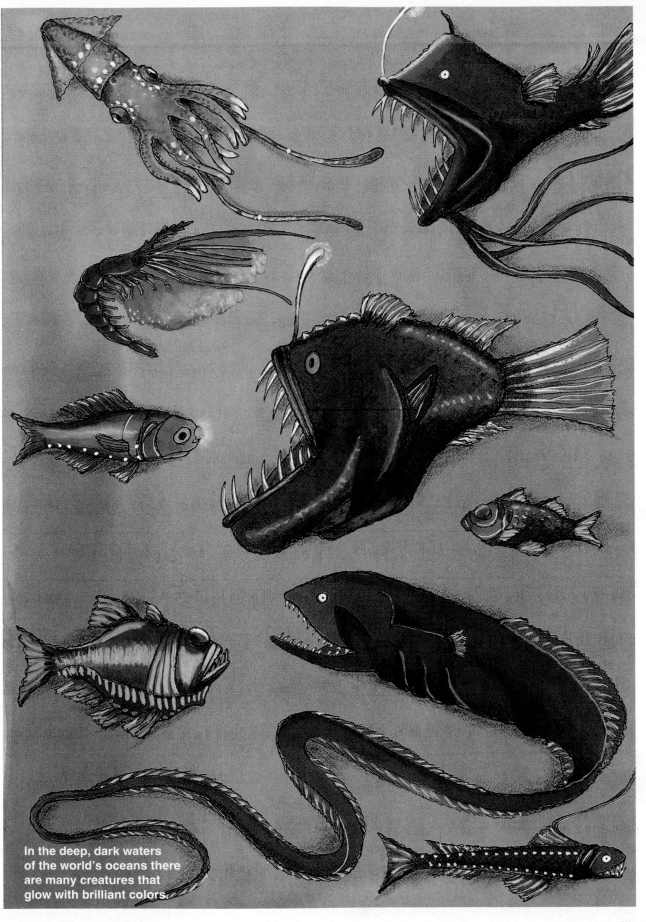

In the deep, dark waters of the world's oceans there are many creatures that glow with brilliant colors.

Barnacles

If you have ever spent a day at the seashore you have probably seen barnacles. They fasten themselves to rocks, pieces of driftwood, the shells of other sea creatures, even to hard-packed sand. Scientists studying a beach in the tropics figured that in one ½-mile (805 meter) stretch there were a thousand million of these little animals. A barnacle can survive wherever water will carry microscopic bits of food, such as algae and the tiny eggs of other creatures, to its mouth.

There are more than 200 kinds of barnacles. Some barnacle shells are shaped like miniature volcanoes, some are flatter. The tiniest barnacles are no bigger than the period at the end of this sentence, the largest measure 6 inches (15 centimeters) across. Barnacles are crustaceans, like crabs and lobsters. This means they have jointed bodies, without backbones, encased in hard outer shells. There are no male and female barnacles. All adults can lay eggs, each producing as many as 30,000 young every year.

The funny thing about a barnacle is that, as soon as it hatches, it sets about looking for a suitable home, and, once it has found one, it never moves again. It doesn't seem as if such a stationary little shellfish would be much of a bother, does it? Yet, of all the creatures that live in the world's oceans, barnacles may be the biggest troublemakers.

Once a barnacle has fastened itself to a surface, it never moves again.

Why are they so troublesome? Because one of their favorite places to live is on the pilings of docks and piers and on the sides and bottoms of boats and ships of all sizes. Removing barnacles costs the owners of boats and ships billions of dollars every year.

Barnacles are difficult to scrape off because they fasten themselves to boats and other surfaces with a self-made super glue that becomes rock hard 15 minutes after a barnacle squirts it out. One little barnacle taking up residence on a boat wouldn't do much harm. But what happens when millions of barnacles attach themselves to a ship's hull? Instead of having a smooth surface that lets the ship glide smoothly through the water, it carries a rough load of barnacles that can make it more difficult to steer. This extra burden of barnacles can also cut a small boat's speed in half.

It seems that barnacles can stick to anything and everything, even the sleek, slippery skin of whales. If you ever see a whale with bumpy, gray-white patches on its body, chances are that, for the rest of its life, it's going to be carrying around a load of pesky barnacle hitchhikers.

People who own boats don't like barnacles. It's not easy to scrape them off.

Corals

The most massive structure on Earth built by humans is the Great Wall of China. It is so huge that it can be seen from far out in space. Yet on our planet there is something even larger that was made by living creatures. Not by people, but by small sea creatures, each no bigger than the nail on your little finger. These amazing little animals, called coral polyps, built the Great Barrier Reef off the coast of Australia. It is an underwater island of coral, 1,250 miles (2,012 kilometers) long! The reef-building coral polyps, which may have been building the reef for a million years, are still at work on it.

Each little polyp is a small fleshy tube that looks more like a plant than an animal. In fact, for many years people thought they were plants, since they stay in one place, never moving from it. The top of the tube is fringed with waving tentacles that guide food to the opening, or mouth, in the center of the top of the tube.

The polyp draws calcium out of seawater and uses it to make a limestone bowl, or cup, around the lower half of its body. Millions of these limestone cups become joined together. As polyps die, new polyps form more limestone on top of the old structure. It branches out in many forms and directions. If you were to dive down to a coral reef you could imagine you were in a fairy landscape with mountains, valleys, tunnels, pillars, castles, flowers, shrubs, and trees.

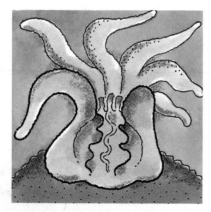

A coral polyp looks more like a plant than an animal.

Divers must be careful not to damage the fragile forms of coral reefs.

This tropical fish lives in a coral reef, a place as colorful as itself.

GLOSSARY

algae Rootless plants, such as seaweed, that grow in water or damp places.

biologist A scientist who studies plants and animals.

calcium carbonate A substance found mainly in limestone, marble, chalk, bones, teeth, and shells.

crustacean An animal with a hard outer shell, no backbone, and a body divided into sections. Crabs, lobsters, shrimp, and barnacles are crustaceans.

fin A winglike organ on the body of a fish or other sea creature. Fins help these animals swim, turn, and balance.

fish A cold-blooded animal that lives in water and has a backbone, gills for breathing, fins, and, usually, scales.

flipper A broad, flat body part that helps certain animals swim.

Great Barrier Reef A coral reef off the coast of north-eastern Australia.

Gulf Stream A warm current in the Atlantic Ocean that flows from the Gulf of Mexico to the shores of northern Europe.

limestone Rock that consists mainly of calcium carbonate.

mammal An animal with a backbone and, in the case of females, glands that produce milk for their young.

mollusk A spineless animal with a soft body that is, in most instances, partly enclosed in a shell. Octopuses, squids, clams, oysters, and snails are mollusks.

29

There are many coral reefs in Earth's oceans. They are all in warm seas, like the Caribbean, or the waters off Florida or the Bahamas. That is because the coral polyps need the help of a certain kind of algae to live and do their construction work, and this algae lives only in warm, shallow water where sunlight helps its growth.

You may think that a reef made of limestone would be drab and gray. Or maybe you picture a coral reef as being the color we call coral. There is coral that is that rosy-pink color, but it is not the kind that reefs are made of. Actually the reefs made by coral polyps come in a dazzling variety of colors. They can be rosy, all right, but they can also be purple, green, yellow, or brilliant orange.

Adding the most color of all to a coral reef are the bright tropical fish and other creatures that make the reef their home. No other environment in the world's oceans contains so many kinds of life. Niches give small creatures a safe place to hide from their predators. Caves and overhanging ledges provide larger animals, such as octopuses, and even sharks, a good place from which to watch for prey.

A coral reef is very delicate and easily damaged. Careless divers or the dragging anchors of boats often break off pieces of branching coral. Sediment can smother polyps, and oil spills and wastes dumped into the oceans can kill polyps and the creatures who live in or near the wonderful structures they have built. That is why it is so important that we have laws that protect our beautiful coral reefs.

Australia's Great Barrier Reef contains many fascinating shapes, among them that of this fan coral.

One of the many kinds of branching corals found in the waters off Bermuda.

Polyps live in colonies that slowly create huge coral reefs.

nipper An organ of an animal used in biting, pinching, or holding.

photophore A body organ that creates and gives off light.

plankton Microscopic plants and animals that live in both seawater and freshwater.

polyp A small flowerlike water animal that has, at the top of a tube-shaped body, a mouth fringed with tentacles.

reef A ridge of sand or rock in shallow water.

sediment Any matter that, in water, settles to the bottom.

shellfish Any creature that lives in water and has a shell.

sponge A sea animal that looks like a plant and is often mistaken for one because it grows in one place. The skeletons of sponges are porous and can hold a lot of water.

submersible A small submarine, commonly used by scientists for underwater study and exploration.

tentacles Armlike parts of the body of certain sea animals. They are used for swimming, feeling, and grasping.

tropics Areas of the Earth, usually hot and humid, lying between the Tropic of Cancer and the Tropic of Capricorn.

Index